From the Peanuts Section: Personality Psychology and Pop Culture

Jon Coley

Published by Jon Coley, 2023.

FROM THE PEANUTS SECTION: PERSONALITY PSYCHOLOGY AND POP CULTURE

First edition. June 16, 2023.

Copyright © 2023 Jon Coley.

ISBN: 979-8223318293

Written by Jon Coley.

In memory of Kevin. You are missed, balloon head.

1. Caveats

MBTI isn't scientific. That's a fair point, but a misunderstood premise. Many in the scientific community (for lack of a better term) point out that the personality typing tool isn't predictive. They're correct. It was created by a mother-daughter team who were American patriots and Carl Jung fans. With World War II ramping up and most men going to fight overseas, the duo used the legendary psychologist's theories to develop a means of helping businesses put new workers (mostly women) in the best possible jobs. Over the decades, the Myers-Briggs Type Indicator has become the most popular personality typing tool. To be clear, it observes and describes; It doesn't claim to predict anything.

There are other systems out there too. As of this writing, the Enneagram is in vogue, and certainly has its merits. The Big Five is currently heralded as the most scientific personality typing system available. This is probably true. They did it the "right way." This system, however, correlates very highly to the MBTI. Socionics is yet another system, but is basically the Russian version of the indicator. MBTI is useful and arguably the most accessible to anyone. That's why I like it. Additionally, disciplines, like neuroscience, are beginning to catch up with and even confirm many Jungian / MBTI theories, though this phenomenon is only in its infancy stages.

I'm an elementary school teacher and an MBTI nerd. While personality typing has a vibrant community, especially on social media, many are reluctant to use it in an educational paradigm. Even MBTI proponents would advise you not to give kids a personality test. I would have to agree. Kids' personalities are developing and changing over time. It is not until late adolescence or early adulthood that the human personality truly comes together and cements. Moreover, one certainly should not artificially foist a personality on a young person. That having been said, a teacher can find the principles behind MBTI more than useful. This book is merely meant to be a guide for teachers, explaining general student behaviors, and perhaps giving some insights as to why kids do the crazy things they do. These personality principles are meant to be a general roadmap of the mind.

I remember my first year teaching. My principal hired me showed me my room one month after school started. The next day, although I was supposed to have two days to prepare, he brought the kids in from the overflow of other classrooms and told me to teach. That is exactly what I did, or tried to do, anyway. I shudder to think what I put those poor kids through as I learned the ropes. A road map would have been helpful.

I bet you're thinking, "Hold on. I thought this book was supposed to be fun, not some teaching book." Rest assured, there are only a couple of paragraphs per chapter on education. All the rest is psychology and pop culture oriented.

This book is divided into twenty chapters, including this one. The next chapter will be an overview of how the MBTI system works. The third chapter is about the four temperaments, which would be most valuable for teachers of younger kids. The next sixteen chapters are about each personality type. Some articles from my old blog, Jon Coley Word Worker, have been inserted in most chapters in order to make the featured type more vivid.

I abhor books that are written like term papers, so footnotes and parenthetical citations will not be included. For now, let it be said that the information in this book comes from the likes of Carl Jung, Elizabeth Meyers-Briggs, David Kiersey, Charles Schultz, and the MBTI community. I'm not affiliated with the Peanuts Franchise, the Myer-Briggs, or any of the other sources mentioned in this book in any way. I'm just a fan who likes writing about these things because I think more people should know about them. I'll be sharing my knowledge of personality typing the way I understand it with one very important caveat, I could be wrong. That being said, I don't think I am.

2.Theory

Okay, it's nuts and bolts time. There are two parts to the psychological theory behind the Myers Briggs Type Indicator. The first part refers to preferences. This is where all the letters come from. The second, and more important part, is the set of cognitive functions. This set thinking patterns is the roadmap to your brain. Essentially, the four letters of your personality type are a key that opens up an App with a dashboard that shows the basics of how your brain works, like a schematic. It describes how your personality is put together.

So what do the letters stand for? There are two basic ways people take in information. Likewise, there are two basic ways that decisions are made. These four pathways can be focused on the outer world or in one's inner world. So, those with mathematical mindsets have probably come up with the magical number eight (2+2=4 and 2x4=8). This is absolutely correct. However, humans only have so much capacity, so only four of those eight functions are used on a daily basis. Not only that, but the top two functions are the most dominant of all. This will be discussed in the cognitive functions part of this chapter.

Now we turn back to the preferences. Humans are habitual creatures by nature. Most of these habits cement early on. One would think that these preferences could easily be changed. This is not so. It's like your hand dominance. You are either left or right handed. Sure you can write with your non-dominant hand, but the results wouldn't be the same. (Okay all you supposedly ambidextrous people out there, we'll have nothing from the peanuts section.) The MBTI looks at these preferences through personality tests and other observations, then assigns a four letter personality type.

Again, what do the letters stand for? Here we go. The two basic ways of taking in information are Sensing and iNtuiting. The two ways of making decisions are Thinking and Feeling. The two ways of approaching the world are Perceiving and Judging. Finally, the two ways of focusing are Introversion and Extroversion. So we have eight capital letters to choose from when selecting the four in a given personality type. There are sixteen personality types in the system, and one chapter will be dedicated to each of them. Here's a quick list of them all below:

ISTP ISTJ INFP INFJ INTP INTJ ISFJ ISFP ESFP ESFJ ESTP ESTJ ENFP ENFJ ENTP ENTJ

So a breakdown of one or two of the personality types would look something like this:

ISTP = Introvert-Sensor-Thinker-Perceiver

ENFJ = Extrovert-iNtuitive-Feeler-Judger

It must be stated that there are many misconceptions concerning personality types. If you're a Sensor, that does not mean you don't have iNtuition. If you're iNtuitive, that does not mean that you have can't Sense details. If you're a Perceiver, that doesn't mean you don't Judge. If you're a Judger, it doesn't mean you don't Perceive. And by the way, being a Judger in the MBTI world doesn't mean that you're judgmental. All Thinkers Feel, and all Feelers Think too. Perhaps the biggest misconception of all would be the difference between Introverts and Extroverts. These words don't have the same meaning as they do in the general lexicon. Introverts aren't necessarily quiet and shy. Extroverts aren't necessarily outgoing. These terms actually refer to what's more real to people. If your inner world is more real to you, you're an Introvert. If your outer world is more real, you're an Extrovert. There are no Ambiverts in the MBTI system, though there are in other typing systems, like the Big Five. This doesn't mean that you can't have traits of both Extroversion and Introversion, though. In fact, everyone does. Finally, it must be emphatically stated that your personality type is not a box that you must be pigeonholed into. Your type is simply a way of showing your thinking and living patterns. There are more than seven billion people in the world, and all of them are different and unique.

Okay, now the fun part, the cognitive functions. The four letters of the personality type are actually a key of sorts. They tell you about the cognitive functions in your cognitive stack. In other words, they describe your habitual thinking modalities. There's a cool little system used to decode the four letters, but it reads like stereo instructions. I mean, who even has a stereo anymore? With that in mind, it would be far more interesting to discuss the eight functions, so here goes nothing.

There are two perceiving functions and two judging functions. Each can have an inward or outward focus. Thus we have two plus two times two, which equals eight. The two perceiving functions are Sensing and iNtuition. The two judging functions are Thinking and Feeling. When you add the inward (introverted) and outward (extroverted) focus, you get this nifty little list below.

Introverted Sensing (Si)

Extroverted Sensing (Se)

Introverted iNtuition (Ni)

Extroverted iNtuition (Ne)

Introverted Feeling (Fi)

Extroverted Feeling (Fe)

Introverted Thinking (Ti)

Extroverted Thinking (Te)

These eight functions and their placement in your stack (habitual thinking) make your personality. The top four are active and detectable to the trained eye. The bottom four go into what Jung called the shadow. We all have one, a dark side. There is some controversy here, but there is controversy in all personality typing, so it goes with the territory. Anyway, the top four functions, and especially the top two, are what make you unique and different. Once again, this does not mean that you are the same as all the other people who have your personality type. It means that you have similar habitual thinking patterns.

Instead of defining, it would be better to describe the functions. They do have definitions, but they are more like territory markers. One behavior is more Se. Another is more Ni. Plus, the functions are developed to greater and lesser extents depending on their place in the stack. With this in mind, descriptors are given for each cognitive function below.

Introverted Thinking (Ti) - focused inward, logical, understands systems and how things work, good at classifying and analyzing, efficient, fair, principled efficient

Extroverted Thinking (Te) - focused outward, logical, understands how to organize the outside world (things and people) and make them work, effective, fair

Extroverted Feeling (Fe) - focused on the outside world, the feelings and values of the tribe, the ambience of the setting

Introverted Feeling (Fi) - focused on inner core values and feelings, accepts or rejects values as part of the self

Introverted Sensing (Si) - inward focus on concrete details, heavily reliant on memory, takes in surroundings in real time and subconsciously compares them to the past or to the ideal

Extroverted Sensing (Se) - outward focus on concrete details, takes in information through the senses, very much in the present, heavily anchored in reality

Introverted iNtuition (Ni) inward focus on patterns, advanced pattern recognition, able to mentally project abstract ideas into the future

Extroverted iNtuition (Ne) outward focus on patterns, easily makes connections to multiple things in the world that would seem to be random

The above descriptions are fast and loose. There are multiple articles written about each one in scholarly psychology journals and on the world wide web. My intention was to simply give an overview of the cognitive functions in order to make it easier to understand how they can contribute to a personality. The truth is that these functions ebb and flow and affect each other within each human being. They are difficult to define because people are difficult to define. Once again, we come back to the concept of the road map. Perhaps, though, a voyage would be a better analogy. Let's go.

So you've got a brain. The brain has four active cognitive functions that make up your personality. The primary function, the first in your stack, is the captain of the ship. What it says goes. The secondary function is the navigator. It takes the captain's orders and keeps the ship moving in the right direction. The tertiary function is the crew. It has its own job to do and does it well, but isn't in charge of the big decisions. It has time to look out over the side of the boat from time to time too, providing a novel view. Then there is the passenger. The inferior function is just along for the ride. It doesn't take part in any decisions, but it will certainly let everybody know if something goes wrong. Finally, the other four inactive functions are the cargo. They sit in the dark and don't do anything in particular, but they are definitely there. One of those pieces of cargo is in a mysterious box. No one has ever looked into it. This is the seventh function. It's known as the blindspot. It could be something completely harmless, but it could be like nitroglycerin, just waiting to blow a hole in the hull. Yes, we all have that dark side in our personality.

Dramatics aside, that's the theory behind MBTI in a nutshell. Now a little theory from me. I believe dealing with children through this lens would be helpful for any teacher. You don't have to type kids. In fact, I wouldn't. You can, however, understand them better. That's why I present to you Exhibit A, the work of Charles Schultz. The Peanuts franchise has been delighting children and adults for generations now. But why? It's just a silly comic strip and some animated shows about kids in modern suburbia. The reason is that the characters are so multidimensional and incredibly authentic. It wasn't until I started becoming interested in personality theory that I discovered just how authentic those characters are.

The next chapter will cover some of Keirsey's work on the temperaments, but every chapter after that will look at each personality type in depth. Most of those will have an excerpt from my personal blog, quite a few of which will highlight a Peanuts character. A few posts highlight characters from other well know works as well. If, by chance, there is no blog post, a complete profile will be provided. No type will be left behind.

3. Temperaments

David Keirsey's book, Please Understand Me II, looked at MBTI from the perspective of a behaviorist. There are plenty of dissenters, but that is always to be expected with the study of personality. His description of the four temperaments, however, are quite useful, especially for educators. Keirsey looked at the age old problem of nature versus nurture. He found that two of the four personality type letters were nature and two were nurture. In other words people were born with half of their personality, and the rest developed as they grew. It was the innate parts that he referred to as the four temperaments. They are listed below.

SP SJ NF NT

In effect, a person would be born as an SP, or an XSXP, and grow up to be one of the four following personality types - ISTP, ISFP, ESTP, ESFP. They were born with the Sensor and Perceiver proclivities and either became an Introvert or Extrovert and a Thinker or Feeler over time. This personality would fully congeal in early adulthood. Likewise an SJ, or XSXJ, would become one of these four personality types - ISFJ, ESFJ, ISTJ, ESTJ. The next temperament, NF or XNFX would grow to become these personality types - INFP, ENFP, INFJ, ENFJ. The final temperament is NT, or XNTX. These are the four personality types stemming from this rarest temperament - INTP, ENTP, INTJ, ENTJ.

The four temperaments can be observed in early childhood, thus kindergarten through fifth grade teachers may find this information helpful. The following paragraphs are brief descriptions, not definitions, of each personality temperament.

The most common temperament is the SJ, called the Guardians by Keirsey. These are detail oriented, concrete thinkers who prefer a structured approach to life. They like their routines and rules and expect others to follow them too. Kindergarten teachers would recognize these kids immediately.

The second most common temperament is the SP, which Keirsey called the Artisans. While as detail oriented and concrete thinking as the Guardians, Artisans prefer a more flexible approach to life. They are not as worried about the rules and routines as their counterparts. They are not necessarily rebellious in nature, but Artisans have a deep love of freedom and individuality. Teachers often find these kids exploring the playground, climbing trees, digging in the dirt, and taking every chance they get to have some kind of (often destructive) fun.

The second rarest temperament is the NF group, or the Idealists. These people are abstract thinkers and are big picture oriented. They prize values and cooperative thinking over logic. Their approach to life may be structured or flexible, depending on the specific type. These are the five year olds that come to the teacher to report how one kid hurt another child's feelings or let the teacher know that another student isn't feeling well.

The rarest of the four temperaments are the Rationalists, or the NT's. These people are abstract thinkers that prize logic in their decision making. They may have a flexible or structured approach to life, depending on their specific type. One type of Rationalist is the classic nerd (INTP), but there are plenty of other rationalists. If a kid doesn't mind arguing or debating with a teacher, just for the heck of it, he/she is probably a Rationalist.

There are varying numbers all over the internet and in psychological literature on personality concerning the commonality or rarity of personality types. It's difficult to narrow them down exactly, so I've decided to give you my ballpark numbers based on my experience as a teacher and an MBTI nerd. Basically, about sixty percent of the population is born Guardian, perhaps twenty-five percent would be

Artisans, up to ten percent would be Idealists, and around five percent are Rationalists. Again, this is pure conjecture on my part, but I feel confident with those numbers based on my experience.

4. The ISTP

The ISTP is known as the Crafter or the Virtuoso. These are Introverts who are more concrete and logical in their thinking. They love freedom and independence. I'm a fan of the ISTP type because I'm one of them. Being patriotic to your own personality type is totally a thing in the MBTI community, by the way. The ISTP is in the Artisan temperament group, and is known for being reserved, yet sometimes surprisingly spontaneous.

A good example of an ISTP is the Peanuts character, Schroeder. Therefore, this will be the first post from my blog in this book. Without further adieu...

A Very Awkward Post

To be honest, I've been putting this post off. If you've been wondering (doubtful) why I haven't yet posted about Schroeder, it's because we share the same personality type. While I'm very comfortable being an ISTP like Charles Schultz' young piano playing virtuoso, I'm not so comfortable writing about him because it's like writing about myself. If I try to portray only the cool things about him, I may seem to be a bit of a bragger. If I only discuss the awkward things about him, it will be – awkward. But since I know quite a bit more about this type than the others, I'm going to stick to the character as close as possible, and perhaps dispel any myths (not egotistical at all) surrounding this type.

ISTP stands for Introverted-Sensor-Thinker-Perceiver. Introverts recharge their psychological batteries by having alone time. Sensors are more detail oriented people as opposed to intuitive minded people, who prefer going by their gut and focusing on patterns. Thinkers prefer to make decisions objectively based on logic instead of feelings and and values. Finally, perceivers prefer to live their lives leaving room for flexibility and spontaneity, as opposed to judgers, who much prefer planning and organizing. The ISTP is given the nicknames of the mechanic, crafter, or virtuoso.

So young Schroeder is an ISTP and a virtuoso. Anyone who knows this character immediately pictures him hunched down over his piano. He's very much an in-the-moment person who is very focused on the task at hand. Some more detail oriented people may have noticed that there is almost never any sheet music in front of him. That's because he, like most ISTP's, is focused on the tool or instrument he's currently using. Much like fellow ISTP, AC/DC's Angus Young, Schroeder is more interested in discovering what he can with the tools at his disposal (nothing from the peanuts section, guitar snobs; the man plays from his gut). He's always got some groupies hanging around, especially Lucy. There are plenty of scenes in the comic strip in which there are more than one of the girl characters at his house while he is playing Beethoven. Yet he is not Mr. Popular (like the ESFP).

The other place that Schroeder is commonly seen is on the ball field. He's Charlie Brown's catcher. This is in all likelihood not an accident. While every position on the team is important, there is no game without the catcher. The ISTP's second cognitive function, extraverted sensing, in step with his primary function, introverted thinking, is the perfect recipe for a very good athlete. The catcher keeps the game going and helps the pitcher decide the best strategy to take out the batter. All this communication takes place without a word spoken between the two players. On top of that, the catcher is the last line of defense between the runner and home plate. So Schroeder has to be Johnny-on-spot when things go wrong. This zone is the ISTP wheelhouse.

So what's it like being a sports icon rock star sex symbol? I honestly have no idea. But being an ISTP, I do know where these stereotypes (important in MBTI speak) come from. We are supposed to be attractive to the opposite gender, like Clint Eastwood, Ashton Kutcher, Scarlett Johansson, or Kristen Stewart (all ISTP's, according to some in the personality community). Celebrities aside, I believe I know where this stereotype comes from. Schroeder is a good example too. The girls are comfortable around him. Being an introvert, he is not as forward as other Extroverted guys. Also, ISTP's like people. Even crabby Lucy is welcome to hang out with him. As for the (somewhat rare) female ISTP, imagine the appeal of a girl who is comfortable talking knowledgeably with the guys about things they care about, but is still all girl. Many girls try to fake that, but the ISTP doesn't.

Sports wise, I was the best benchwarmer around. This was mainly because I'm knock-kneed and flat-footed. Plus I was six feet tall weighing a whopping one hundred thirty-five pounds. As one may surmise, team sports was never my forte. But I discovered I had the knack for karate when I was in high school. Soon after that I discovered the wonder of playing the guitar. Nowadays I'm partial to woodworking and writing. I may not be an Aston Kutcher or Clint Eastwood, but I have my own Lucy. I sure wish I still had that blonde hair like Schroeder's, though.

*

That was a pretty good post, if I do say so myself. Unfortunately, it didn't give the cognitive stack of the ISTP. This will read like stereo instructions, but we may as well get it over with. Let's dive into my brain.

I'm an ISTP. The preferences were already discussed in the blogpost, but now we have the key to opening my cognitive stack. The first step is to look at the two middle letters, ST. These are my main Perceiving and Judging functions, respectively (remember PJ's to keep it in order). Now, look at the last letter. The P in my preferences signifies that my main Perceiving function is Extroverted, so my S is Se, or Extraverted Sensing.

Now we go back and forth in dichotomies. If the S is Extraverted, the T will be Introverted, or Ti. So my top two cognitive functions have been discovered, but what is their order? For that we look at the first letter, the I. I'm an Introvert, so my first function is Introverted Thinking, or Ti. Now it's just a matter of stacking the functions.

I run a tight ship (not really). My captain function is Ti. It's the one in charge. My navigator function is Se, the second in command and the one who makes sure I know where I am. Now, the opposite of Sensing is iNtuition, so my crew function is Introverted iNtuition, or Ni. This takes care of many day to day minor tasks and has a different view than my first two functions. The opposite of Thinking is Feeling, so my passenger function is Fe, or Extraverted Feeling. This function isn't in charge of anything, but it's certainly present and willing to make its opinions known. Deep down in the hull of the ship is the cargo. These functions aren't active, but they are still a part of the voyage. One of them is a little dangerous, the blind spot. It would be the seventh of the eight functions, but an easier way to recognize it would be to simply change the focus of your third, or crew function. For me, I just have to change my Ni to Ne. That's my blindspot, my kryptonite, my dangerous cargo. There will be more on blindspots in a later chapter.

ISTP - Ti, Se, Ni, Fe

There it is in all its glory, the map to my brain. Believe it or not, it says a lot about me and my behavior. I lead with Ti, which means I'm a logical thinker. My secondary function is Se, which means I pay attention to my surroundings more than most (but not as much as the ESTP). My third function is Ni, which means I'm not necessarily a big picture thinker, but I can focus on problems and recognize important patterns when the need arises. My last active function is Fe. I'm not a feely kind of guy. I can be quite socially awkward too, but I do recognize and often respond to the feelings and values of others as well as the overall atmosphere in a room. There's more to it, of course. It gets more interesting when you start looking at stereotypes, but this book isn't intended to get that far into the weeds, and there's an entire MBTI community online for that.

5. The ESTP

Also in the Artisan group, the ESTP is more outgoing than his/her ISTP cousins. Known as The Negotiator, this personality type is the wheeler dealer of the MBTI world. Charles Schultz had two ESTP's, Snoopy and Franklin. Yes, one is a dog, but you have to admit he's got quite a personality.

Beguiling Beagle

Snoopy is an ESTP. Believe it or not, he is even easier to type than some of the other "human" characters in the Peanuts franchise by Charles Schultz. This outgoing, yet cool dog has such a big personality that he's become every bit of a cultural icon as Charlie Brown himself. In many ways, he's the star of the show.

The ESTP personality type is known for being action oriented. ESTP's are the first type (whether they know it or not) thought of in the "Bro Culture" phenomenon that is so often portrayed in the media. Known as the negotiator, the ESTP is known for making things happen. They are high energy people who aren't afraid to jump into the fray at a second's notice. In school, they are the kids (more often boys) who are looking around trying to find something to do, or even some trouble to get into. While they can be tough-minded and aren't afraid of conflict, they are often warm hearted and open individuals who make friends easily and truly enjoy the company of others. They are the ultimate in-the-moment people.

Here's the breakdown. The E means extraverted, S means sensing, T means thinking, and P means perceiving. An extraverted person gets psychological energy from being around other people. A sensor is a person who is more detail oriented as opposed to someone who is more possibility and pattern focused. A thinker is a person who values logic over feelings. This doesn't mean that they are unfeeling, but they make decisions based on facts. Finally, a perceiver is a person who prefers flexibility and openness over planning and structure.

Does this sound like Snoopy? Well, he definitely likes to be with others. He's really more the neighborhood dog for the whole Peanuts gang. One can easily conjure up images of Snoopy dancing and playing joyfully with the group. He is action oriented and adventurous, whether he's fighting the Red Baron or boxing with Lucy. Logic is more important to him than the feelings of others. While easier to see in the comic strip with thought balloons, this trait can be illustrated in the cartoons too. Take note how he handles Lucy in a confrontation, giving her a big wet kiss. It certainly wasn't to make her feel better. He even took on the part of Peppermint Patty's tough as nails ice skating coach. The images of him holding his dog bowl before Charlie Brown or trying to get into public institutions (no dogs allowed) show his negotiating skills. He's certainly warm and open. After all, a beagle is a hunting dog, yet Snoopy's best friend is a little yellow bird.

Exceptional Personality

One Peanuts character seems to be a chameleon. In many of the specials, he's pretty quiet. He's more talkative in the comic strips, but still difficult to figure out. There is a reason for this. Most of Charles Schultz' beloved characters were based on real people. Franklin, the first black kid in the Peanuts universe, was created out of whole cloth.

A school teacher wrote Charles Schultz a letter, in which she lamented that it was a shame that there were no relatable characters for black children on television. He agreed, thus Franklin was born. Charlie Brown first meets him on vacation at the beach where he learns that Franklin's father is overseas serving in Vietnam.

So Franklin was first much like Charlie Brown himself, probably an ISFJ. Later, as the character developed and became loved by both fans and Schultz himself, his personality changed. He was more outgoing. He became more like everyone's best friend, Snoopy, an ESTP. This isn't as evident in many of the TV shows, but is pretty plain in the comic strips and many Peanuts children's books. The best example of this is when he negotiates a deal with the older kids who were pushing Peppermint Patty (of all people) off the ice for their hockey game. He and Snoopy made quite the team.

It can be argued that this character was the token minority. I don't disagree, but it was brave of Schultz to create him at the time. This blog is apolitical. Feel free to think about this what you will. The point is that Franklin, while having different origins than the other characters, still grew into an authentic, well developed personality that can be described by MBTI. This is a testament to good writing that makes for prolific, even iconic, material.

*

All right, you got a two-for-one deal in this chapter. Again, it is important to discuss the ESTP's cognitive stack. The one letter difference between ISTP and ESTP is important. The cognitive functions are the same, but in another order. This creates a completely different personality type.

The captain function of the ESTP is Extraverted Sensing (Se). It is always taking in the surroundings, including the behaviors of all the other ships around it. The navigator function is Introverted thinking (Ti), which makes logical sense of the captain's orders. The crew function is Fe, which pays attention to morale, feelings, and values, especially those of the other ships in the area. The passenger function is Introverted iNtuition (Ni). This function doesn't get to make many decisions, but can make its insights well known from time to time. The rest of the functions are down in the hold below deck, the cargo functions. Introverted Feeling (Fi) is the most volatile cargo hidden deep in the shadows, the blind spot. This doesn't mean that the ESTP lacks core values, only that values are meant to be shared by the tribe at large to this personality type.

ESTP - Se, Ti, Fe, Ni

When teachers send kids out to recess, the ESTP's are the ones running out as fast as they can. They are the ones climbing on the monkey bars and jumping off from the tallest heights. There are usually a few ISTP's with them, but it's easy to tell the difference. These groups are usually boys, but there are always a few girls too.

6. The ISFP

Can you believe it? When I wrote this post, I included the cognitive stack. That makes things easier for me, which is always a good thing. There will still be a short, teacher oriented review afterward, though.

Sweet Surrender

So there I was sitting in a multi grade level meeting. I had just figured out a colleague's personality type. MBTI had become an obsession because I knew deep down in my heart that my developmental psychology background, which was basically an equivalent to a minor in an early childhood education major, really missed the boat when it came to Jungian psychology. Carl Jung was just a passing footnote in my training. More on that some other time. Where was I? Oh yeah, so my colleague was an ISFP, known as THE ARTIST in the MBTI community. She was not the first one to have this type, nor would she be the last among my coworkers. But here's the thing. In this meeting, there were almost twenty people (rounding up). We were all sitting randomly in the classroom, only loosely grouped by grade level. That was when I noticed that all four of the ISFP's that I had typed were sitting in a perfect diagonal line in relation to each other. It was a surreal moment (it doesn't take much for me). These women knew each other, of course, but they didn't know each other's personality types, and they were in different grade level groups too. Yet there they were, making a quiet, artistic statement in an otherwise chaotic (as far as seating goes) setting.

The ISFP is, once again, known as THE ARTIST. A good description/ mantra for this type would be, "Still waters run deep." They are introverts, thus the still waters, with a highly developed sense of self from an emotional standpoint, thus the running deep. There preferences are Introversion-Sensing-Feeling-Perceiving. Their decisions are often made based on strong personal values and they approach the world with an open attitude. The ISFP's I know have a wide range of passions – dog rescue, calligraphy, and even studying moths, just to name a few. Often inspired by the world around them, ISFP's interact with it through an in-depth, emotional, highly focused lens. Aesthetics are usually important to them because they truly appreciate the beauty our world has to offer.

The most famous ISFP I know of would be the singer/songwriter, John Denver. I'm dating myself here, but readers over forty probably just giggled a little. If you're a younger reader, for Pete's sake check out his music. There are two types of people in the world – those who love John Denver, and those who won't admit it. By the way, the title of this post is the title of one of his songs. It has nothing to do with ISFP's. I just love the tune.

The cognitive stack of the ISFP is as follows: Introverted Feeling (Fi), Extroverted Sensing (Se), Introverted Intuition (Ni), and Extroverted thinking (Te). Fi is their primary, or driver, cognitive function. It's like a filter that says, "This is me, that's not me." It's based on deep, profound emotional imprints and personal values. The navigator, or secondary, function is Se. This is what allows them to connect with the outside world in an in-the-moment way. Their tertiary, or passenger function is Ni, which allows them to see patterns, usually having to do with their personal passions. Finally, their inferior function, the tag along, is their least developed. Te allows them to organize things, people, systems in logical ways. This is often the function they should work on for self growth. It's how they can achieve "alpha mode."

Statistically speaking, you know some ISFP's. These are good people to have in your circle. Value their friendship, because they will value the good things about you. They may be a little quiet sometimes, but there's a lot more to them than meets the eye.

*

In the post above, I discussed the driver, navigator, passenger, and tag along functions. This is the car model. I first heard about this model online from a Husband Wife Team called Personality Hacker. Their website by the same name is a good resource for any MBTI nerd, and I'm a fan of their podcast. My ship model works pretty much in the same way, but I like the vivid, more exciting, voyage/journey illustration it provides to the mind's eye (at least to mine, anyway).

I didn't mention the blindspot, though. The ISFP's blindspot is Extroverted iNtuition (Ne). If you start brainstorming and rambling on about random possibilities and connections, they will quickly fade into the background, if not leave the room altogether.

ISFP - Fi, Se, Ni, Te

A teacher would know these Artists anywhere. Yes, they like rough and tumble play just as much as any Artisan, but they are sensitive souls. They love to create and to enjoy the finer things in life from a young age. There will be another post on the difference between the ISTP and ISFP included in the final chapter of this book. Incidentally, the ISTP and ISFP share the same blind spot, Extroverted iNtuition (Ne), which will also be discussed in another post later.

*

Update: Since this book was first published, I discovered that I had left out a very important Peanuts character, Woodstock. I believe that this lovable yellow bird is an ISFP.

7. The ESFP

The Entertainer, the social butterfly, the life of the party - these are just some of the titles bestowed on the ESFP. The next blog post covers the preferences and the cognitive stack. The only thing it doesn't cover is the blindspot, Introverted Thinking (Ti). Logic is not their strong suit, at least not when dealing with abstract ideas, like higher mathematics. This doesn't mean that they can't make the grade, only that it is incredibly tedious to them. You're probably not going to find an ESFP sitting down to listen to a university lecture on physics. You may, however, find her/him emceeing the event and making it quite entertaining.

Naturally

Her name is Freida, not the little red haired girl. She was the one with the naturally curly hair. Now that that's out of the way, it's easier to understand why her personality was so easy to type. Charles Schultz' Peanuts character was named after a real life friend he met in an art class named Freida (the friend, not the class). She was probably an ESFP, because the one with the naturally curly hair certainly is.

The ESFP in the Meyers Briggs system (MBTI) is also known as the Entertainer. This type is outgoing and fun loving. People with this personality type are also independent and friendly. But before we go any further, some negative stereotypes of this kind of personality are usually misleading. For instance, because they are usually snappy dressers (old man term, I know) they are often considered vain. Because they are usually the life of the party, they are sometimes considered to be attention hogs. This is unfortunate, because it usually isn't true at all.

The ESFP abbreviation stands for Extraverted-Sensor-Feeler-Perceiver. The entertainer is one of the most extraverted, outward focused, outgoing kinds of person there is. They are sensors, which means they are detail oriented as opposed to being people who view the world in terms of possibilities and patterns (the intuitives). Being feelers, the ESFP's make decisions based on values and feelings as opposed to thinkers who make decisions based on logic. Perceivers prefer to experience the outside world by leaving room for flexibility and freedom, unlike judgers who prefer organization and planning.

The cognitive stack for the ESFP is Se-Fi-Te-Ni. Using the Road Trip model (your brain in a car), we get a glimpse into the working mind of the Entertainer. The driver is extraverted sensing (Se). This cognitive function takes in massive amounts of detail and data from the outside world in real time. People with Se as a lead function are COMPLETELY in the moment. They can pick up on the most minute things, like body language and micro expressions, far better than most. Their navigator function is introverted feeling (Fi). Fi is a values oriented function that focuses on one's personal beliefs and feelings. People with this cognitive function being high in their stack are the epitome of the old adage, "Be true to yourself." The passenger (10 year old in the back seat) function for this type is extraverted thinking (Te). This function uses logic to organize the outside world, to create systems, to make things (and people) the way they ought to be so they can work better. The final, what I call the tag-along, function (toddler riding in a car seat) is introverted intuition. This least developed cognitive function looks to the future and focuses inwardly on patterns, possibilities, and gut feelings.

So Freida, with the naturally curly hair, is outgoing and fun loving. When she first befriended Linus, he had to admit that he didn't know what was going on in class because she talked to him so much. She is always in the moment and knows how to have fun, like when she's chatting with the usually crabby Lucy on the ball field instead of playing her position. Although, to be fair she's not the one who needs to be traded (thanks to her Se) in "Lucy Must Be Traded, Charlie Brown." She's always cracking a joke, even though it's the same one about her hair. She's determined to help Snoopy hunt rabbits (Te). Beagles are hunting dogs, after all. She always tries to look her best for everyone else. Freida is a great example of a young ESFP.

Growing up, my best friend was an ESFP. I currently work with two ESFP's who are wonderful people. This is probably why I feel the need to explain more about this oftentimes overlooked and undervalued personality type. Because they are outgoing and are usually the center of attention, some may think they are vain or shallow. Nothing could be further from the truth. Sure, they get a lot of attention, but this is because they are giving a lot of attention to others. Because they try to look their best, they are called vain. In all actuality these people are the opposite of narcissistic. They are usually trying to make their world a better place in little ways by having fun. What's wrong with that?

*

ESFP - Se, Fi, Te, Ni

If you're a teacher, you know these kids. They are chatty and fun loving. ESFP's are great when it comes to oral presentations and group work, as long as they can stay on task. There's never a dull moment with them around.

8. The INFP

We're switching gears now, moving on from the Artisans to the Idealists. Our first Idealist is the INFP, or the Healer. The next featured blog post is about everybody's favorite blanket carrying, thumb sucking sidekick, Linus Van Pelt.

Not So Complex

When they see Charles Schultz' Peanuts character, Linus Van Pelt, many people think he has a "Linus Complex." But many in the MBTI community probably see all the stereotype traits of an INFP. This personality type, while not as famous as the INFJ, is not all that uncommon. It's very interesting that Charles Shultz paired these two types as siblings (Lucy being the INFJ) in his comic strip. So this thumb sucking, blanket hugging kid makes for a fascinating study (to me at least).

INFP stands for Introverted, iNtuitive, Feeling, and Perceiving. This personality type has been given "The Healer" as a monicker, a nickname that fits Linus perfectly. He is introverted because he has a rich inner world. The wheels are always turning, so to speak. The NF is a powerful combination which allows Linus to understand the feelings of others on a deep level. He is able to follow patterns of human behavior and go with his gut feelings in any given situation. Unlike his sister, Lucy, he has a more open and flexible approach to life (P).

So how does this play out? Linus is Charlie Brown's supportive friend who is always available to listen to him. He encourages him and helps him when he can. In his novel approach to life, it was Linus who famously wrote encouraging letters to Santa Claus instead of telling him what he wanted for Christmas. Even his beloved blanket is a mark of the INFP, who is known to be sentimental to things that have enriched his/

her life. On a different note, INFP's can be quite stubborn once they latch on to a personal belief, hence The Great Pumpkin.

Also, you may have noticed that this character is not at all infantile in spite of his blanket and thumb sucking trademark habits. Likewise, he's not the least bit fearful or as insecure as one may expect. He even used his blanket to teach some bullies a lesson in one Peanuts cartoon. Again, true to his personality type, he was called to action to protect someone else, not himself. INFP's are supportive souls who see the potential in others and love to see it come to fruition. In that regard, Charlie Brown is lucky to have such a good friend, complex or not.

*

This post left out the cognitive stack, so I've got a little bit of work to do. Let's see what life is like aboard the USS Linus aka the INFP.

The captain of cognitive functions is Introverted Feeling (Fi), so the INFP makes most decisions based on internal values. The navigator cognitive function is Extroverted iNtuition (Ne), or outward focused possibilities, connections, and patterns. The crew cognitive function is Introverted Sensing (Si), which heavily depends on memory and the way things were (or ought to be). The passenger cognitive function is Extroverted Thinking (Te). It doesn't have much say in the decisions being made for the ship, but still makes it's opinions known concerning what should be done and how to do it. Deep below decks is the cargo, the shadow functions. Even deeper in the hold is the blindspot, Extraverted Sensing (Se). To me, this is interesting. It signifies that the INFP's blind spot is the outside world! Don't get me wrong. I'm not saying that INFP's are in La-La-Land, only that they have an incredibly rich inner word.

INFP - Fi, Ne, Si, Te

Teachers, this kid is the day dreamer in your class, but not the ADHD one. This kid has a lot going on in his/her mind. The child may slip through the cracks in many ways, but will suddenly stand out as a passionate leader of the class when an important cause comes up, like The Great Pumpkin.

9. ENFP

The ENFP is called the Champion. While being a much more outgoing member of Idealist temperament, this type can be charming and usually quite charismatic. As the blog post below will illustrate, Charles Schultz' champion isn't afraid to get down and dirty.

Fresh Air?

There are some people who don't like ENFP's. They find them annoying and too unpredictable. These people are, in a word, jerks. ENFP's are fantastic people. I'm a big fan of this personality type. Odds are that you are too. After all, Charles Shultz' character, Pig-Pen has been rated as the fifth most popular Peanuts character.

First, I need to clear up some confusion. Being an ENFP doesn't mean that you are continually surrounded by a cloud of dirt. It does, however, mean that you can get into something so whole-heartedly and enthusiastically that you may have neglected to put on your make up or you don't mind that your clothes have become disheveled. Also, some in the MBTI community have labeled Pig-Pen as an ISTP because of his dirty overalls. Sorry, not even close. Pig-Pen is one of the most extraverted characters in the franchise. True, an ISTP doesn't mind getting his hands dirty. But our (I'm an ISTP) secondary extraverted sensing can feel every drop of sweat and every gritty piece of dirt on every part of our bodies while we're working. When not working, we clean up, and usually pretty well if I do say so myself. But to be clear, it isn't Pig-Pen's dirt cloud that makes him an ENFP. It's his energetic, yet easygoing and positive attitude. That's why we love him and why you probably love the ENFP's in your life.

The term ENFP stands for Extraverted-iNtuitive-Feeler-Perceiver. Extraversion is the quality of being psychologically charged by being around others. Intuition is the quality of perceiving the world through the lens of patterns, possibilities, and gut feelings. Feelers make decisions by instinctively considering values and feeling of others on the team over using logic. Finally, being a perceiver means that you prefer to leave space for flexibility instead of spending too much time planning and keeping routines.

The ENFP is in the Idealist temperament (NF). There are four temperaments that people are (probably) born with. This temperament is known for caring for fellow man (like Ghandi - INFJ). While the INFJ is the most extraverted introvert, the ENFP is the most introverted extrovert. They get so high (for lack of better word) being with other people that they need to spend time alone to cool down and recenter (but not recharge like an introvert). These people are fun, witty, creative, friendly, and enthusiastic. In short, they are a blast to be around.

So young Pigpen may be surrounded by a cloud of dust, but his personality is a breath of fresh air. He is not a poor vision of poverty and hopelessness, but a dynamo of creativity and joy. That's why he is so loved by the peanuts gang and so loved by you.

*

There you have it, Pigpen is Charlie Brown's Champion. Sure, he's a little rough around the edges, but his personality shines through. The post did not cover the cognitive functions, so let's see what life is like on board the good ship ENFP.

The captain of the ship is Extraverted iNtuition (Ne), so it's always looking about for possibilities and is recognizing patterns that many may not see. The navigator is Introverted Feeling (Fi), which stabilizes the captain's seemingly random decisions and perceptions with a strong sense of inner values. The crew is Extroverted Thinking (Te), which knows how to get things done, which is perhaps a good thing with such a crazy captain at the helm. The passenger is Introverted Sensing (Si), so it's busy thinking about how things used to be back when the voyage first began. The cargo functions are down below with the blindspot, Introverted Thinking (Ti) locked deep in the hold. This suggests that you shouldn't bother the captain of this ship with facts and logic, those are just details!

ENFP - Ne, Fi, Te, Si

As a teacher, you'll see the ENFP being a bubbly, creative little whirlwind. She/he will care about the feelings of others, but will also be a dynamo of activity. When dealing with this kid, fasten your seatbelt!

10. The INTP

This is a nerd. No, really, the INTP is the classic nerd stereotype. That doesn't necessarily mean pocket protectors and glasses, but it does suggest a love and devotion to data. Yes, there really are people like that, and you should get to them. This the first type in The Rationalist Temperament. Charles Schultz' character, Marcy, is a great example of this personality type.

Lord Have Marcy

Let's face it, Marcy is a nerd. The word, nerd, was first used by Dr. Seuss, but his illustration did not stick. Charles Schultz Peanuts character arguably did more to illustrate this now ubiquitous term in the English language (as well as others). Believe it or not, this data driven character is a legitimate MBTI personality type – the INTP.

To be fair, being an INTP doesn't mean you're going to wear glasses (though many of them do). It doesn't mean you are going to wear pocket protectors and braces either. But the natural cognitive functions of the INTP, nicknamed the Architect, do lend themselves to classic nerd iconography (probably not the right word here, but I like it). But if you are an INTP, you are a bit of a nerd, and that's a good thing. After all, Bill Gates famously advised students, "Be good to nerds. You're probably going to work for one someday."

The abbreviation, INTP, stands for Introverted-iNtuitive-Thinker-Perceiver. An introverted person recharges his psychological battery by being alone, and doesn't mind working alone. An intuitive person relies on gut feelings and is good at recognizing possibilities and patterns. They are often mentally stimulated by big concepts and theoretical thinking. Thinkers prefer to make decisions by using logic. They separate themselves and any emotions they may have from the situation at hand

and make decisions about it objectively. Perceivers prefer to approach life leaving room for flexibility. They are not overly obsessed with scheduling and planning. If this paragraph got a little tedious to you, you're probably not a nerd, I mean INTP.

So Marcy is definitely introverted. She prefers hanging around with and having a deeper relationship with one friend, Peppermint Patty. She's certainly logical too, but not just with her schoolwork. She used very concrete logic when punching out her bully/would-be suitor at camp because she logically concluded that she was not a lamb chop. Marcy is brutally honest with Peppermint Patty (by the way, she knows her friend is a girl) not just by calling her sir, but when opening up to the possibility that she might be wrong in given situations, right in line with the intuitive aspects of her personality. Finally, Marcy is happy to let her friend drive the agenda. They are always doing what Patty wants to do, just like any good perceiver.

There are some surprising things about INTP's (nerds) that most don't recognize right away. First, they are not necessarily afraid of bullies. Many mistake their social awkwardness, due to their low ranking extraverted feeling in their cognitive stack, for fear. This is not the case. INTP's are grouped into the Rationalist temperament. They know who their enemies are and, barring threat of physical harm (usually), they're not afraid to take action against them. It's just that they are going to be smart about it.

Surprisingly, many INTP's have a great appreciation for romance. Marcy was the one who began referring to Charlie Brown and Peppermint Patty as Charles and Priscilla in the Thanksgiving special. In a conversation at work, my INTP colleague said that she married her husband because he was so thoughtful and romantic. People will always surprise you.

*

Just for poops and cackles, let's have another blog post covering this iconic personality type. I wrote a couple of book reviews on my blog for a great fantasy author, Charlie Holmberg. The main character of one of her books is a great example of an INTP.

One More for Charlie

I recently wrote a book review post about Charlie Holmberg's Paper Magician Series. The three books are a fun and fascinating read. They also illustrate the ESTJ personality through the main character, Ceony. But her work deserves one more review (from me anyway). Another book she published, THE PLASTIC MAGICIAN, is written in that fantastic materials magic world. This one, however, features a new heroine, Alvie. I was delighted when I realized that this new character wasn't just a rehash of Ceony. Alvie is unquestionably an INTP. This, to my mind, is a great credit to her writing. She told a great story with an interesting new character whose attributes are well thought out.

The INTP, Alvie, is a young American magician's apprentice who gets the opportunity to study abroad in England with the famous polymaker, Magician Praff. This INTP is the classic nerd. She's introverted, easily distracted, has a proclivity and even love for math and data, and is socially awkward. Yet she is lovable and compelling.

If you are an INTP or know and love one, give this book a read.

So let's see what life is like on board the USS INTP, nicknamed The Architect. The captain of this ship is Introverted Thinking (Ti). Decisions are made through facts and logic. The navigator is that scatter brained (just kidding, this function is my blindspot) Extroverted iNtuition (Ne), always throwing out seemingly random, but actually connected possibilities and patterns of direction. The crew is Introverted Sensing (Si), which works to keep the ship together, but is always remembering how things have fallen apart in the past. The passenger is Extroverted Feeling (Fe), which notices morale and lets everybody on the ship know how awkward things are. The shadow functions are deep below decks, and the dreaded blindspot is Extroverted Sensing (Se), which is the reason why nerds are so often considered gawky and spastic.

INTP - Ti, Ne, Si, Fe

Okay, I went a little over the top with this description, but it's easier to paint a picture that way. A teacher will recognize this kid. It's the nerd in the classroom. I'm not saying this to be mean, I'm probably going to end up working for one of these kids some day.

11. The ENTP

I don't have a Peanuts character to present as an example of this personality type. Instead, I have a blog post about a personal friend I've known since our freshman year of high school. This is also another book review. Sean is quite a prolific writer.

Bizarre

Let's face it ENTP's are bizarre people. Oh, they're good folks and usually fun to be around. But they're just weird. I submit exhibit A – NIGHT PEOPLE by Sean Gilbert.

Before I continue, full disclosure. I've known the author personally for decades. He's a good friend of mine. He's written many books over the years, all bizarre in their own way. This one, though, is the perfect glimpse into the mind of an ENTP. Sure there are a lot of weird things going on in the plot. You've got devils, contrarian floating heads, somewhat of a mermaid-succubus-human love triangle, and armed civil war re-enactor battles. But the truly bizarre thing in the book is the lead character's cavalier, yet cynical attitude. This attitude, intellectual as well as emotional, is a trademark of the ENTP.

The ENTP is the Extraverted-iNtuitive-thinker-perceiver personality type in the Meyers-Briggs system (MBTI), nicknamed The Debater. While the author may certainly be one of these, the main character in NIGHT PEOPLE definitely is. This is a fun book to read with interesting short stories and over the top supernatural fun. It's great for Halloween. But in the streets of Savannah, Georgia, it's just par for the course.

Note: The movie version would probably be rated PG-13 for strong language. This isn't a criticism at all. But since I write fiction for kids and he doesn't, I didn't want any confusion.

*

It's cognitive function time. Let's see what it's like on the USS Sean, I mean ENTP. The captain of the ship is Extraverted iNtuition (Ne). He's always looking out for and discovering new possibilities, and catching on to patterns that are often unseen by others too. The navigator is Introverted Thinking (Ti). Somebody's got to be logical on this crazy vessel. The crew is Extroverted Feeling (Fe). This is good for keeping morale high and for getting along with other ships. The passenger is Introverted Sensing (Si). He's not a big decision maker, but he's good for sitting around and telling stories about days gone by. The other functions are in the cargo hold. Buried the deepest of all is the blindspot, Introverted Feeling (Fi). This doesn't signify that the ENTP doesn't have his/her own personal values, only that using them is not the way to get through to this personality type. Their values are generally the shared values of the society, especially those with logical standing.

ENTP - Ne, Ti, Fe, Si

The ENTP's nickname is The Debater. That's how a teacher will recognize this kid in the classroom too. They will talk to anybody about anything. This doesn't mean that they are unruly, only more willing to participate in the discussion. They are sometimes known as the devil's advocate. I wonder why.

12. The ISTJ

Though I personally know several ISTJ's (five immediately come to mind), the Peanuts gallery seems to be ISTJ free. Known as The Inspectors, ISTJ's are good, loyal friends to have. The next post is about an unlikely and often mistyped ISTJ character written by J.K. Rowling, the one and only Professor Snape. The YouTube Channel, The Heart of Michi, was where I first made this discovery. Most would disagree with the host, Michelle, about this. I, however, do not. And since this is my book, the detractors are wrong.

What'd You Say about Snape?

Ah, Professor Snape, the hated, yet beloved Harry Potter character. He was written by the great JK Rowling and portrayed in film perfectly by the late Alan Rickman. So much of the Harry Potter saga hinges on this one character in ways that no one would come to expect. The one word catch phrase, "Always" was seared into the hearts of millions. A new respect for strict teachers was found in those hearts too (That may be wishful thinking on my part). The MBTI community loves the planning and plotting from this INTJ icon. The thing is, he's not an INTJ.

Wait, what? That's right, I said it. Snape is an ISTJ. Shocking, right? As an MBTI geek and Harry Potter fanboy, I just assumed the community at large was correct. He fit the dark, brooding stereotypes very well. Here's where the stereotypes fail, though they are generally necessary in the MBTI community.

Before I make the Snape ISTJ case, I have to admit that I didn't figure this out on my own. There's a YouTube channel called HEART OF MICHI that I was watching. She, Michelle, was ranking fictional INTJ characters. The lowest ranking was "Not an INTJ." I thought she was going to put Gregory House there, because I don't think he's an INTJ either, but no. She put Snape there and proclaimed he was probably an ISTJ because his prime motivation was definitely related to Introverted Sensing (Si). The lightbulb was lit.

It all came together. His "Always" motivation was his love for Harry's mother. He died looking into Harry's eyes (Surely that's not a spoiler, right?), because they were his mother's inheritance. This is Si, or the memory driven cognitive function, all the way. What about all that planning and potion making? Well, he didn't plan anything. That was all Dumbledore. While he loved potions, his true passion was Defense Against the Dark Arts.

Harry Potter himself actually summed it up best when he mocked Voldemort, telling him that Snape was Dumbledore's man all along. Snape is the ultimate, self sacrificing ISTJ soldier. Not only that, he was a stickler for the rules, especially when dealing with HP. If that's not ISTJ, nothing is. So now maybe you can enjoy this literary and cinematic character in a new light.

*

Okay ISTJ Harry Potter fans, you've got a new hero. I truly think it is a compliment. This is a character with a heart of gold, tough and loyal. The post left a lot of information out, though. Here's the preferences breakdown. ISTJ stands for Introvert-Sensor-Thinker-Judger. This is a person who needs time alone for psychological recharge. The Inspector is detail oriented and logical. Finally, the ISTJ prefers to approach life in a structured (stick to the rules) way.

Now we can look at the cognitive stack on board the USS ISTJ. The captain of the ship is Introverted Sensing (Si). This captain is always concerned about the way things ought to be. The navigator is Extroverted Thinking (Te), always organizing and creating systems and rules for all to follow. The crew is Introverted Feeling (Fi), making things work based on personal values and standards. The passenger is Extroverted iNtuition (Ne), who doesn't get much say in the decision making, but let's all kinds of possibilities be known to everyone else. The rest of the functions are below decks with Extraverted Feeling (Fe) being the blindspot, so Morale and the comfort of the group may be a little awkward from time to time.

ISTJ - Si, Te, Fi, Ne

Teachers, don't look for the kid with long, greasy hair and black robes. That's just Snape. The ISTJ could look like anyone, but will act like a rule follower who expects everyone else to follow the rules too. This doesn't make them tattle tales, though. The ISTJ is more likely to confront the rule breaker one on one, so pay attention, these are great kids to have in the classroom. In fact, one way to spot this kid is to take note of the students who ignore the others and even give them derisive looks when they're not supposed to be talking. Yes, those kids really do exist.

13. The ESTJ

This personality type is called The Manager. ESTJ's are natural leaders, especially in small groups. They know how to get things done. There is one character that Charles Schultz introduced into the Peanuts cannon who embodies this personality type, Peppermint Patty.

It's All About the Clothes

It was really the clothes that did it. I wasn't sure sure whether she was an ENTJ or ESTJ. She is definitely extraverted, probably the most outgoing character in the whole franchise. She was definitely a judger. After all, there is a certain way that things must be done. But her clothing was what clenched it. ENTJ's are known to be snappy dressers (does anyone actually say that anymore?). They personify the old saying, "Dress for the job you want, not the one you have." But she wore a green, untucked shirt, shorts and sandals all the time. That settled it, ESTJ, the Manager.

I'm writing about the beloved, freckle faced tomboy, Peppermint Patty, from Charles Schultz' Peanuts franchise. This bold, in your face character is the epitome of the ESTJ. The Manager is the monicker they are known by in MBTI circles. This is due to their primary cognitive function, extraverted thinking. This function is logical in nature, but oriented toward the outside world. It's an organizing, planning, commanding function. ESTJ's are good at setting up systems and setting up logistics, which are ideal traits for getting things done. Their second function is introverted sensing, which is a memory function that is continually focused on the way things ought to be (for lack of a better phrase). This combination of thinking is a manager in the making.

How does this play out for Peppermint Patty? She is definitely extraverted, probably the most outgoing friend Charlie Brown has. The Thanksgiving special shows how much of a people person she is with all the networking, dealing, setting up and (self) inviting she does. Her introverted sensing is on display as she is disapprovingly taking in the odd holiday dinner being served to her by Snoopy and Woodstock. Her love of tradition is apparent when she asks where the turkey, stuffing, and mashed potatoes are. Finally, her introverted feeling, the last function in her cognitive stack, is made manifest after her friend, Marcy, reproves her behavior and sets her straight. She is harder on herself than anyone else is. But she bounces back quickly, not wanting to play "lovers games" with that "sly dog" Chuck.

I personally know four ESTJ's, two of them at work, one at church, and one I grew up with. Believe me when I say that they are just as entertaining as "Chuck, Old Boy's" Peppermint Patty. By the way, their clothing tells the tale too. It's not that they are bad dressers. But we can't all be ENTJ's.

*

ESTJ's are Extroverted-Sensor-Thinker-Judgers. They are outgoing, detail oriented dynamos. They are all about planning ahead and they love it when a good plan comes together. One thing that is often missed about this personality type is that all that planning, organizing, and bossing around of others (elephant in the room statement) often comes from a good place. It usually comes from the heart. It's their way of contributing to the group, their way of helping.

On board the USS ESTJ, the captain is Extraverted Thinking (Te). This function organizes the outside world as fairly and logically as possible, regardless of feelings. The navigator is Introverted Sensing (Si), the memory function that is always concerned with the way things were or ought to be. The crew is Extroverted iNtuition (Ne), the function that notices seemingly random possibilities and patterns. The passenger is Introverted Feeling (Fi), which doesn't get to make many decisions, but has a strong sense of inner values. In its own way, it can be the ship's anchor. The other functions are deep in the hold, and the among those is Introverted iNtuition (Ni), the blindspot. This indicates that ESTJ's are more about breadth as opposed to depth, not that they can't be deep people. They are more interested in making things work and keeping that ship sailing right.

ESTJ - Te, Si, Ne, Fi

Teachers, when you put kids into groups, look for the group that is working super efficiently on its own. It is probably being lead by an ESTJ. They are usually very good students, even though there are many comic strips with Peppermint Patty sleeping in class. I think that what Schultz was trying to say was that she was a better leader than follower.

14. The ISFJ

This is the most common personality type. Even so, about ninety percent of the population is not this type, just for some perspective. That having been said, it's time to type the star of the show.

Face it Kid, Your Head is Just Too Darn Big

Years ago one of my friends found one of his baby pictures and shared it with us. Well, actually it was more of a toddler picture. We all laughed, including him, because his head was HUGE. To be fair, the rest of his body did eventually catch up and he no longer looks like a genetically engineered mutant. But in that picture his noggin looked like a balloon on a string.

My friend is an ISFJ. This is one of the sixteen personality types in the MBTI system. It is, cranium volume aside, a fairly common type consisting of a little over ten percent of the population depending on where you research it (heads up Wikipedia). The ISFJ is known as THE DEFENDER. It is one of the four Guardian temperaments. This personality type not only belongs to my large headed friend, but it also belongs to everyone's favorite blockhead, Charlie Brown. Charlie Brown is a Defender? Defensive, sure. But a Defender? In a word, yes. He is a person who defends the way things ought to be.

Taking a look at the ISFJ preferences, we have Introversion, Sensor, Feeling, and Judging. Introverts need alone time to recharge their psychological batteries. Too much social interaction wears them out. This doesn't mean that they are shy or antisocial, but they must strike a balance between their social and alone time. The Sensing preference is detail oriented and directly depends on the five senses. While we all do this, the difference is that sensors take in information like this far more often than they are following hunches or listening to their gut, which is more like what an iNtuitive person would prefer. A Feeler makes decisions based on values and emotions instead of logic. This doesn't mean that they are not logical, but their go-to method is more harmony focused instead of taking objective positions. Finally, the Judging preference refers to how they interact with the outside world. It doesn't mean that they judge others too much (though some certainly may), but that they need to have things scheduled and planned. Flexibility and spontaneity are not their cup of tea.

If this doesn't paint a picture of Charles Schultz' primary Peanuts character for you, moving from the preferences to the COGNITIVE STACK probably will. The preferences (what ISFJ stands for) are like a key opening the door to a (very) simplified schematic of the human brain. The Cognitive stack is a list of the four cognitive functions used by each personality type. The first two, the primary and secondary, are like the driver and navigator of your brain – This is your brain, this is your brain on a road trip. Charlie Brown's top two functions are Introverted Sensing (Si) and Extraverted Feeling (Fe). Si takes in information from the environment in real time and automatically compares it to preconceived and previously experienced ideals and situations. This past-oriented function depends heavily on memory. So mega-memory equals mega-noggin? Fe is focused on the values shared by the community at large and the overall morale of a given situation or environment. It is harmony focused. An Fe user is easily agitated when harmony is out of balance.

So how is this all related to Charlie Brown? His catch phrase is, "Good Grief!" This is because his lead Si is always recognizing how things are out-of-whack. He has an excellent memory and an expectation for the way things should be. So he knows how his dog should act, but Snoopy insists on sleeping on top of his doghouse. The Fe function makes him very (overly) sensitive to the feelings and perceived thoughts of others, like the little redhead girl. He is a Defender, however. He's the one taking on the responsibility of leading and pitching for the most ragtag baseball team in history (Bad News Bears aside). He's also the only Peanuts character to specifically defend his friend, Pigpen (Google it).

Long story short, Charlie Brown may be a blockhead, but he's a great guy. He's a true defender of his friends and loved ones. He's a staunch protector of the way things ought to be (even Christmas and sad little trees). While you probably would not want to be him, the world is definitely better with him in it. And we are all better off with our blockheaded ISFJ's too.

*

Charlie Brown (and probably Charles Schultz himself) is an ISFJ, known as The Defender. I wrote a little about his cognitive stack, but didn't cover it fully in the post, so let's look at life aboard the USS ISFJ.

The captain of the ship is Introverted Sensing (Si), which relies heavily on memory and is primarily concerned with the way things ought to be. The navigator is Extroverted Feeling (Fe), always concerned about the morale of the harbor and how everyone is feeling. The crew is Introverted Thinking (Ti), the logical decision makers milling about the deck trying to understand how this ship works. The passenger is Extroverted iNtuition (Ne), shouting out wild possibilities and patterns to anyone who will listen. Below decks is the cargo, the shadow functions. The blindspot is Extroverted Thinking, which indicates that Charlie Brown doesn't react well when being told what to do. That doesn't mean he's rebellious, though. It just means he's going to have a lot of inner qualms about it.

ISFJ = Si, Fe, Ti, Ne

I don't think all ISFJ's necessarily have large craniums, so teachers should look out for the kids who are worried about, and focused on, taking care of others instead. They are not likely to come to the teacher with problems, but usually prefer to help their friends out on a one-on-one basis. They are introverts after all. These kids can "fall through the cracks" because they are far more likely to complain to themselves than to others. "Good Grief," is more of a mantra to this personality type than even they would know. I don't want to make it sound like there's something wrong with the ISFJ. This is a perfectly healthy personality type to have, and it's the most common of the sixteen. It's just easier to point out their problems, because that's the simplest way to recognize them.

15. The ESFJ

I only have one post on my blog having anything to do with ESFJ's, and it's more about jumpers, which really won't be helpful here. The only Peanuts character that may be an ESFJ is Patty (not Peppermint). I cannot say for sure, because she became more obscure as the comic strip developed over time. So we're just going to get right down to it in this chapter and talk about The Provider.

Think supermom. Also think Mr. Mom. The ESFJ is known as the Provider, as stated before, but is also known as The Supporter. They live to be helpful ... and to gossip. This is a little unfair of me to say, because I'm an ISTP, who would label almost any kind of small talk as gossip. The ESFJ is all about the tribe, be they family or coworkers.

Their preferences are Extroverted-Sensor-Feeler-Judger. Being extroverts, they are very much involved with group dynamics. These are outgoing individuals. They are also detail oriented people who make their decisions based on tribal values and morale. People with this personality type prefer to approach life in a structured, stable manner.

Now we can look at the cognitive stack on board the USS ESFJ. The captain of the ship is Extroverted Feeling (Fe), which is looking out for the welfare of all the other ships in the harbor. The navigator is Introverted Sensing (Si), the memory function, remembering all kinds of details about those other ships. The crew is Extroverted iNtuition (Ne), running around noticing all kinds of random possibilities and seeing patterns everywhere. The passenger is Introverted Thinking (Ti), the most logical function on the boat that has the least say in what's happening on it. The cargo functions are below decks where we find the blindspot, Introverted iNtuition (Ni). This indicates that the ESFJ doesn't relate to sitting still and analyzing patterns of one specific topic. They like to keep things moving.

ESFJ - Fe, Si, Ne, Ti

Teachers know these kids by how they are constantly doing things for others. While quite talkative, they can also be selfless in nature. In short, they have big mouths and big hearts.

16. The INFJ

Now we come to the rarest personality type, the INFJ. Known as The Counsellor, this type is someone that even strangers feel completely comfortable sitting down with and telling her/him their whole life story. Now which Peanuts character has people coming to her for advice? I'll give you a hint. They usually have to pay her a nickel.

Lucy, I Have Some Explaining to Do

This iconic image below (my blog had some illustrations) of Charles Shultz' character, Lucy, in his beloved Peanuts franchise is the epitome of the INFJ. (Sorry, no pictures in this book, but you should know what she looks like by now.) Some may disagree with me on this, but it's a free country and they have the right to be wrong. Now, some may not see past her aggressive attitude and the way she is prone to pick on the other characters. INFJ's are supposed to be sages, not bullies. Well, if you get past that, you can see Shultz' remarkable insight into the human personality. It's one of the reasons his work has been so successful and will continue to be remembered for generations.

So what makes Lucy an INFJ? First of all, the nickname of this personality type is "The Counsellor." And there she is, offering her two cents to the world for only a nickel. Most readers laugh, as they were supposed to, at the irony of the child's play gag. But true Peanuts fans have probably noticed that the other characters are more than willing to take her up on the offer. People feel comfortable about telling INFJ's everything, their whole life stories. The joke is usually in the simplified, eccentric advice she gives, but she is usually not wrong. Real life INFJ's have the uncanny ability to predict human behaviors thanks to their dominant introverted intuition.

Why is Lucy so grumpy? Her patience is often tried by "blockheads." INFJ's are introverts. They need time away from others to recharge their mental energy. This doesn't mean that they are reclusive, but they do get frustrated with others who don't see the patterns they so easily pick up. This doesn't mean that they are always grumpy, though. They can be fun loving and playful (trust me, I know).

Speaking of being playful, let's talk about athletics. The INFJ has inferior (as in forth on cognitive stack) Extraverted Sensing (Se). This means that they are not usually the MVP of the game, as illustrated in the cartoon, "Lucy Must be Traded, Charlie Brown." But just because athletic prowess doesn't come naturally to them, that doesn't mean they are all clumsy. Any healthy INFJ can become as good as any other player on the team with practice. And with all that introverted intuition, they can pull that football away just before Charlie Brown attempts to kick it every single time. This also means that they can appreciate good strategy, so it's not at all surprising that an INFJ girl would be a football fan.

One last thing (or set of things) about the INFJ. The F stands for feeling. They truly feel for others in a deep way. If you're upset, they're upset, even if no words have passed between you. Likewise, if you are in your zone (like Schroeder on his piano), they feel that too, and may appreciate it even more than you do. Everyone needs an INFJ in their lives. This blockhead is lucky enough to be married to one.

By the way, INFJ's don't hate dogs. But beagles are stinky. And you have to admit, Snoopy is really weird.

*

So let's look at life aboard the USS INFJ. The captain of the ship is Introverted iNtuition (Ni), always looking through the spy glass into the future on the far horizon. The navigator is Extroverted Feeling (Fe), paying attention to the morale, values, and the very mood of the tribe, whether wanting to or not. The Crew is Introverted Thinking (Ti), analyzing smaller details in a logical way and checking out how things work. The passenger is Extroverted Sensing (Se), which observes the reality of it all on board the ship, but doesn't have much to do with any decisions being made. Below decks, the cargo functions are stored with the blindspot being Extroverted Thinking (Te). Don't ever bother telling an INFJ what to do. It's a complete waste of time. Trust me.

INFJ - Ni, Fe, Ti, Se

To be honest, you may not have an INFJ in your classroom. In a grade level of one hundred kids, there may only be one or two of them. If you have a grumpy kid, like Lucy, who's primary reason for being upset is all of the stupid things her classmates are doing to themselves, you may very well have an INFJ. But they may not be grumpy at all. You can also look out for the kid who happens to be all the other kids' go-to person, the one they seek for advice.

17. The ENFJ

Called the Mentor, the ENFJ is an outgoing person who's known for being encouraging to others. I like to think of Ms. Frizzle from The Magic School Bus. With that picture in mind, we can scale it down a little bit in the form of someone's outgoing little sister.

Great Expectations

She was a tough one. I should have recognized it more clearly, because she's the same type as one of my best friends. At first I thought she may be a an ENFP. But the proverbial shoe just didn't fit. Part of the problem was due to psychic projection (woo-woo). Also, she was a younger. Therefore she had less psychologically developed personality. Not to mention the fact that she's a fictional character, which MBTI nerds type all the time for fun, but are often completely wrong. But it was her expectations of others that made the difference. Sally Brown, Charlie's little sister, is an ENFJ.

The ENFJ, also known as THE TEACHER, is one of the sixteen personality types described in the MBTI system. The abbreviation stands for Extraverted-iNtuitive-Feeling-Judging. Sally is definitely extraverted. This is quite easy to see when you compare her to her introverted brother, Charlie Brown. This beloved Charles Schultz character is also intuitive, which means she views the world in terms of larger patterns and possibilities. Feelers, like Sally, make decisions based on values first and logic second. Finally, our little friend is a judger. This means that she prefers planning and security over flexibility.

The personality type, ENFJ, is identified by habitual preferences, but these four letters are also a key to unlocking the cognitive functions. These are basically a highly simplified blueprint of Sally's, and real ENFJs' psyches. Sally's driving function is extraverted feeling (Fe). This function is attuned to the ambience, values, and social customs of the outside world. The navigator function is introverted intuition (Ni), which focuses on the future, possibilities, and patterns. The passenger function (10 year old in the back seat) is Extraverted Sensing (Se). This less developed function takes in the outside world through the senses. It's an in-the-moment function that is more detail oriented. The tag along (toddler in a car seat) function is the least developed in the cognitive stack. In this case, the tag along is Introverted Thinking (Ti), a lone voice of logic crying out in the wilderness.

Sally Brown's Fe is on full display in the Peanuts Movie when she ropes Linus into dancing with her, which completely changes the atmosphere of the school dance. Her Ni is also evident in several ways – making deals to take her neighbors tree at Christmas time, looking to take Charlie Brown's room from him at every turn, getting super crafty for the school talent show. Her not so well developed Se is more subtle. She is no athlete, but she's also a younger character, so this is a bit more of a hidden trait. But for me, the underdeveloped Ti was the deciding factor. Her less developed logic is used, often hilariously, to support her Judger tendencies.

Specifically, It was her Judger tendency of having traditional expectations of others. She expected her brother to take up for her. She expected Linus to produce results during his Great Pumpkin fiasco. She even had high expectations from Snoopy when she told her neighbor to get out of her yard or she would have to sic her dog on him. It was only logical to her that these things should happen.

I'm sure others may have typed Sally differently, and that's okay. They have the right to be wrong. Quite honestly I don't question their MBTI typing abilities at all. I just don't think that they're big Peanuts fans. I've always been fascinated by the depth of these characters and how iconic each one of them are. By the way, that Se can be developed. Plenty of

ENFJ's have become accomplished athletes, but you'd be amazed how many of them are artists too.

*

I did a pretty good job covering the cognitive stack in this post, if I do say so myself. But I did neglect to mention the blindspot. Deep in the hold below decks of the USS ENFJ is Introverted Sensing (Si). Sally, Ms. Frizzle, or any others with the Mentor personality type are not in the least concerned with two things - living in the past and silly rules.

ENFJ - Fe, Ni, Se, Ti

Teachers will see the ENFJ being encouraging to other kids, especially when working in groups. They have colorful personalities in more ways than one. They may get a little loud from time to time, but it's not usually out of defiance. These kids are high on life. Speaking of colorful personalities, both of my ENFJ friends have the same, bold artistic painting style. So if you see a kid slapping color on a canvas with more zeal than the other students, this may a future a Mentor.

18. The INTJ

Nicknamed The Mastermind, the INTJ is often depicted as the evil boss pulling the strings and making the plans. Think James Bond's Dr. No. While it's true that they make plans and pull strings, this doesn't make them evil. Someone has to figure out how to get things done. Movies and books use the INTJ to make characters like Sherlock Holmes nemesis, Moriarty, but real life puts them in all kinds of other roles, even school teachers. In some ways, I think INTJ's are some of the most misunderstood people.

They are Introverted-iNtuitive-Thinker-Judgers. Being Introverts, they need alone time to recharge their psychological batteries. They are in the Rationalist temperament, so they are forward thinkers. They use intuition and logic think abstractly and logically. Since they are Judgers, they prefer a systematic, planned approach to life. It's easy to see how this personality type can be misunderstood. After all, it's the quiet ones you have look out for.

Let's look at the cognitive stack on board the USS INTJ. The captain of this ship is Introverted iNtuition (Ni), always looking out on the horizon, far into the distant future. The navigator is Extroverted Thinking (Te), which keeps all the other ships in the harbor organized. The crew is Introverted Feeling (Fi). Yes, this type has core values! The passenger is Extroverted Sensing (Se), which is paying attention to everything, but doesn't get much say in the decision making. Below decks is the cargo, all the other cognitive functions, called the shadow functions. The blindspot is Extroverted Feeling (Fe), which is probably why the INTJ is so misunderstood. They are not affected or in tune with the ambience, feelings, or values of the tribe. They have their own values and their own plans. By the way, with Ni being the primary cognitive function, they make and carry out plans far into the future. I'm talking about twenty years into the future!

INTJ - Ni, Te, Fi, Se

While not as rare as the INFJ, The Mastermind is pretty scarce population wise. Teachers may not have one of them in their classroom. Most are male. In fact, the female INTJ is rarer than the INFJ. But look out for a quiet kid that doesn't act quite the same as the other students. Perhaps he seems aloof and in his own world. He's probably quite serious in demeanor and not very athletic. He may be in good shape, so to speak, but just won't be very coordinated. Take heart. He's probably a well adjusted, well-meaning INTJ, not a serial killer.

19. The ENTJ

The final of the sixteen types is the ENTJ, called the Executive. This is the big boss. My father-in-law, one of my all time favorite people, happens to be this type, though he doesn't know it (unless he decides to read this book). These people are natural leaders. Like their INTJ cousins, they are in the Rationalist temperament. However, they are far more charismatic and outgoing.

They are Extroverted-iNtuitive-Thinker-Judgers. These extroverts thrive in social situations, but they are also logical, forward thinkers. Being Judgers, they prefer a planned, structured approach to life. It is within these structures, like the military or corporate environments, that they usually shine the brightest.

The captain of the USS ENTJ is Extroverted Thinking (Te), making sure all the ships in the harbor are organized and in good working order. The navigator is Introverted iNtuition (Ni), recognizing patterns and possibilities to prepare for the future. The crew is Extroverted Feeling (Fe), paying attention to the mood, ambience, feelings, of the harbor as a whole. The passenger is Introverted Sensing (Si), which doesn't have much say, but remembers so many good stories from when the ship was first launched into this mighty sea we call life. Below decks the cargo functions are stashed. Hidden deep down is the blindspot, Introverted Feeling (Fi). So while the Executive is a people person, he may have some trouble relating to a few eccentric Bohemians every now and then.

ENTJ - Te, Ni, Fe, Si

Like the ESTJ, teachers will often see the ENTJ taking the reins during group work. The Executive, however, is more opened to possibilities. They are not as detail oriented as their Sensor brethren. This means they often take in more input from the others in the group and build a working system in a more collaborative way. They are usually pretty popular due to their charisma and open nature. But make no mistake, once a decision is made, what they say is what goes.

20. Explanations and Other Randomness

It's a fair question. I stated earlier that personalities develop over time. Younger kids' personalities aren't set. But here's the thing, they will be. If Keirsey is correct, each of those four temperaments will go on to develop in four different ways. My experience as a teacher tells me that sometimes these kids are fully formed personalities. In other words, they have some preferences already, and are leaning toward a specific personality type. While things certainly can change between childhood and adulthood, this knowledge can be helpful for any teacher. It provides a hefty set of arrows for your pedagogical quiver. Educators can use these observations to meet kids where the are.

Teachers can use their knowledge of cognitive functions to better tailor instruction and lesson plans (No, I don't think you should document all that). What's the use in being objective and logical when you've got a room full of feelers (math class aside)? If you have an intuitive thinker, they may be able to help the other kids detect patterns and achieve greater depths of knowledge. And what about blindspots? Maybe the reason you have a personality conflict with a certain kid is because his primary cognitive function happens to be your blindspot, or vice versa.

Now for something completely different. Most of my posts were profiles of Peanuts characters. What can I say? I'm a fan. But my blog had plenty of other MBTI musings, so the rest of this chapter (and book) will consist of those random bits of personality conjecture. This isn't being done to take up literary space, though. Hopefully it will fill in some of the blanks, metaphorically speaking. There are posts explaining the blindspot, the shadow functions, duals, and other personality typing phenomena.

Hopefully this writing will have a positive effect on any educator who reads it (or anyone else for that matter). I truly believe a more in-depth understanding of personality is an incredibly helpful tool for teachers. And any help teachers get would be good for students too.

The Antagonist

As stated in my first post, I like to use personality typing. More specifically, I like to use it to develop my characters. My go-to method is the Meyers-Briggs Type Indicator (MBTI). There is a large community of MBTI enthusiasts out there. To be sure, it also has its detractors. That's all well and good, but I still like to use it in my writing. If it's a major character, he/she probably has a personality type in my mind, and I like to stick to the stereotypes attached to it. This makes the character more authentic to the reader. The antagonist is no exception.

The antagonist in my book, THE CURSE OF MR. M'S CASTLE, is a supernatural creature from Scottish and English folklore called a brownie. The brownie has a type, or part of one at least. Since it is a supernatural creature, one could be forgiven for tweaking this process (I hope). The brownie is almost completely comprised of Introverted Thinking, known as Ti in the MBTI community. So this creature is very logical and calculating. It makes decisions and finds solutions based on cold, hard facts. This is by no means an evil trait. But if left unchecked by a more value oriented function, one could see how this creature could become problematic (especially when dropped in a new environment, a chaotic American elementary school).

In my next book, which I'm currently writing, the antagonist will be another supernatural creature. It is known as a trowe in folklore. Not to be confused with the sea trowe (don't ask), this mound dwelling supernatural creature of Scottish mythology is far more troublesome than the domestic brownie. With that in mind, the main personality function I plan to use for this creature is Extraverted Sensing, or Se. Se is a far more outgoing function and is very sensual (duh) in nature. It is a function that is completely in-the-moment. With that in mind, the trowe promises to be far more action oriented, which will hopefully make for a very fun story.

*

INFJ

One does not write about personality typing without referring to the INFJ. If you go to YouTube, you are sure to find a plethora of INFJ videos. Some are by INFJ's and some are about them. The main reason for this is that it is the rarest personality type in the MBTI system. Everyone thinks they are rare. Everyone wants to be the INFJ. Simply put, no you don't.

This type has a nickname, The Counselor. This is pretty cool. The stereotypes, which are not bad things in the MBTI community, describe the INFJ as the go-to person for everyone else. They are the ones you always feel comfortable talking to and even telling them your whole life story. They are the people who can give you excellent advice, and even when you don't follow it, their predictions almost always come true. They know people. They know you, often better than you know yourself.

If you think you're an INFJ, you're probably wrong. They are exceedingly rare in the population, like around one to three percent rare. These unicorns of the MBTI community are marked by their lead cognitive function, Introverted iNtuition (Ni). This function is often used subconsciously and is always running, sometimes much to the INFJ's chagrin. It picks up patterns and possibilities. It produces strong hunches and gut feelings. You may be thinking that this sounds like you. You have intuition, hunches, and you like to go with your gut. Well, half the population has introverted intuition, but it's not their lead function. It's further down the stack. It's properly pushed down into that dark place where childhood traumas go (stole that line from Modern Family). But for the INFJ this function is the main driver of their personality, and they can't turn it off. They can't not know about you. They can even literally feel the feelings of a complete stranger when she walks into the room!

I'm definitely not an INFJ, and glad of it. I'm perfectly happy to be a little more commonplace. It seems a fair trade to me. So why am I so fascinated by this personality type, you may ask? Well, I'm not an INFJ, but I happen to be married to one. So to my wife I say I love you and you're definitely one of a kind.

*

Blind Spots

I work in an elementary school, but not in the usual teaching capacity. Im part of a four person team in an early intervention program. We are the Notorious EIP! Taking part in a push-in model, we invade all of the classrooms in our school to work with students on their literacy skills. It's been very successful, but working with a team has its own dynamics (and challenges).

Of course, being into personality typing, I've typed them, the whole darn team (ISTP, ISFP, ESFJ, and INTP). Our team is comprised of one extravert and three introverts. In some of our meetings, I've noticed the phenomenon known in Socionics as the blindspot. (Socionics is basically the Russian version of MBTI).

So what is a blindspot? Well, just like the places on the flank of your car that you can't see while driving, personality types have blindspots in regard to cognitive functions. Many in the MBTI community have adopted this concept.

There are eight cognitive functions in the MBTI personality typing system. Each personality type is comprised of four of them. The other four fall into what Jung referred to as the shadow, which is a topic all its own. The seventh cognitive function, which is the third in the shadow, is the blind spot. This is the cognitive function that each personality type just doesn't get or relate to at all. We all have one.

Back to my team, specifically the three introverts. I'm an ISTP. My colleague, whose name may or may not rhyme with Marlene, is an ISFP. While we have two very different types (one letter makes a big difference), we share the same blindspot – Extraverted iNtuition (Ne). This cognitive function has to do with exploring abstract possibilities, continually. I hate it. I like to focus on a quick, simple solution to a problem. Brainstorming is the bane of my intellectual existence. It's like a bug flying around that needs swatting. My colleague is negatively affected by this as well, though more from a values/feeling perspective. To her, these brainstorming sessions are like that giant spider she recently had to kill in her garage with a broom in the wee hours of the morning in near darkness. There is nothing good about that situation.

Well, the other introvert on our team, whose name may or may not rhyme with Mindy, is and INTP. She's all about the Extraverted iNtuition, a brainstorming extraordinaire. Ne is the second highest function in her cognitive stack. In our meetings, if that Ne kicks in, my eyes glaze over. It short circuits my brain. Now don't get me wrong, this cognitive function is important to have in team dynamics. After all, Albert Einstein is believed to be an INTP. Possibilities need to be explored. Somebody's got to do it. I'm not going to do it. My ISFP colleague isn't going to do it. The ESFJ is a story for another post. So to my colleague and friend whose name may or may not rhyme with Mindy, I salute you for coming up with all those possibilities that only you care about.

*

Dualism (A Totally Self Indulgent Post)

Back in the 1990's I was in a rock band. Actually I was in several. But when I think back to that time, I only think of one. We called ourselves I.F. What did that stand for? That depended on what day of the week it was and which one of us you asked. We were what became known as "Alternative Rock," which was popular at the time. There was an entire artistic movement from that era that I don't believe has been given it's due respect, but that's neither here nor there right now.

For a while I believed we were the best band in the world. The world never quite caught on, but enough people did for us to have a great time. The basic lineup was always Chad (lead singer/ guitar), Jack (bassist), Michael (drummer), and myself (guitar). Over the years (yes, we lasted years while most bands lasted weeks), the lineup grew to have the other Jon and Burt (both guitarists) as well as Shane and Stewart (drummer and bassist respectively). The ins and outs of the lineup always enhanced the sound of the band to me. After Jack died and Michael moved to Athens, the ride was over. But it was a blast, and we have more (and probably better) experiences than most rock bands in our area at that time.

But why did it work? Back then I didn't know why the creative dynamics worked so well. Now given what I know about personality types, it makes perfect sense. Our egos, though we certainly had them, never got in the way. I always felt like Chad and I were the creative engine because we came up with most of the songs. But Michael and Jack had full free creative input that helped shape the songs beyond what we ever first conceived. I think the other guys felt that way too.

But back to that creative engine. I believe it worked so well and produced so much material (well over 100 songs at the time) because Chad and I were dual personality types That term comes from Socionics, which is another system related to MBTI. We were exactly opposites. I am Introverted. Chad is Extraverted. I am a sensor. Chad is an iNtuitive. I am a Thinker. Chad is a Feeler. I am a Perceiver. Chad is a Judger. So the two dual personalities (ISTP / ENFJ) worked very well creatively.

If you know your personality type and can type others fairly well, I highly recommend befriending your dual type. You will both very likely be better off for it. This can actually be life changing. Here's an irony for you. Chad's type is sometimes called "The Teacher" and mine "The Mechanic." However, I went on to become a school teacher and Chad likes to rebuild classic cars!

*

You're Not an Ambivert, We All Are

When asked, most people have trouble committing to being introverted or extraverted. Then somehow they find out about being an ambivert. "That's me," they say with a sense of satisfaction in doing away with their own ambivalence. But are they really ambiverts? This is highly doubtful. This ambiguity (okay, I'll take it easy on the assonance) is reinforced by the fact that the answer to this question depends on who you ask.

The Big Five is the most scientifically accepted personality system out there. It is very friendly to statistical nerds, because it was literally born from statistical analysis. Psychologists are probably going to choose this personality assessment over others in their practice. This system allows for ambiversion because it views everything on a spectrum. So when it measures a person's extraversion, and that person is in the middle of the spectrum, you have yourself an ambivert. Great, you're just another statistic. Sarcasm aside, The Big Five is a useful system, but to me and many others it's not as accessible.

MBTI is based on Carl Jung's psychological theories. The Jungian views are not spectrum oriented. They are based on dichotomy, two sides of a coin. Thus we have Extroversion vs. Introversion, Thinking vs. Feeling, iNtuition vs. Sensing, and Judging vs. Perceiving. In this system, there is no ambiversion to be found, but more n that later.

There are reasons to prefer MBTI. My primary reason is its accessibility. Anyone can understand and benefit from using the system. The more you use it, the more accurate it is. It's not a numbers based system. This is why there is a thriving MBTI community out in cyberspace. People who use the system know that there is definitely something to it. (By the way, there are some people trying to apply scientific objectivity to MBTI. Check out the YouTube channel, ObjectivePersonality.)

However, MBTI doesn't ignore ambiversion. It accounts for it in an elegant fashion. Using my personality type, ISTP, one can see how ambiversion is addressed. I am an introvert, as the I in my type abbreviation suggests. This means that the primary function in my cognitive stack is introverted. Mine is Introverted Thinking (Ti) to be exact. In the MBTI system, if your first function is introverted, your secondary function is extroverted. For me that's extraverted sensing (Se). It's in the dichotomy between these two functions where the ambivert is found. For me, I'm usually in introverted mode, thinking and writing or working and building. But in my extroverted mode, I'm in the moment, focused on and taking in the outside world with my senses (Se). At times like these, I'm even communicating with and enjoying being around other people.

So we're all really ambiverts. No one is perfectly in the middle. We all have our situations where we can be more outgoing. We all have our need to be alone. It's just that some of us need these things more than others.

*

Go Ahead and Jump!

No, I'm not reviewing a Van Halen or Pointer Sisters song. I'm finally writing about jumpers. Again, this is probably not what you're thinking. It's not about incredibly useful fashion wear or suicidal bridge dwellers. It's a phenomenon in the MBTI system of personality typing. This post may be 'in the weeds' for most, but I think understanding people is important. And as Granny Weatherwax said, "Magic is easy, but people are hard." (I seriously hope you google her. She's a great character.) So without further delay, let's dive into my jumper story.

I typed a friend and coworker recently as an ESFJ. She was very sure about her preferences, and not on the fence about any of them. When she looked at videos describing her type, they seemed to be a good fit. But when she found out who some other people people were that shared her type, she had doubts. Now, she wasn't being judgmental or mean. She really saw a discrepancy, and I happened to agree with her when I thought about it. At first I went with Occam's Razor and presumed I was wrong. But later on, intuition kicked in. I had typed my first jumper.

Ode to Occam

So what is a jumper? I first came across this term while watching the YouTube channel, ObjectivePersonality. These people work to back up MBTI with more scientific rigor by typing objectively. One thing they discovered was that some people, almost 50% with some types, preferred to switch their second and third functions within their cognitive stacks (told you it was in the weeds). The first and last functions were always nonnegotiable. These people were called jumpers, because their two middle cognitive functions jumped the line.

In the weeds

Back to my friend. She is an ESFJ, but she's a jumper. I like to use the car model to explain the cognitive stack. The typical ESFJ has the following 'brain on a road trip.' Extroverted Feeling (Fe) is the driver.

Introverted Sensing (Si) is the navigator. Extraverted iNtuition (Ne) is the passenger, and Introverted Thinking (Ti) is the tag-along. In a jumper the Ne, which is usually the cognitive function that is like the 10 year old passenger staring out the back car window, becomes the navigator sitting up front with the driver. The Si gets to sit in the back seat and play with the tag-along toddler.

My jumper friend is a little different than other ESFJ's. She's still a Provider, which is the nickname of this type, and still has the Guardian temperament. But she is able to focus more on possibilities (Ne) and use her gut instinct instead of being navigated by memories (Si) and the way things ought to be. The people at the aforementioned YouTube channel don't go into why some people are jumpers, but I believe it a compliment to these people. I think the Jungian MBTI cognition description is the default setting and that these people have developed their lower function more due to life circumstances or positive attitudes and will. In other words, their 10 year passengers have grown up to be trustworthy young adults who are able to help the driver navigate on the road trip of life (Wow, that was incredibly esoteric). But that's just my intuition talking.

*

Dark Times

Every person has a dark side. Carl Jung referred to this as every person's psychic shadow. It's what you know about yourself that you'd rather not admit or even consider. Even the best of us have one. We try to ignore it, but that doesn't make it go away. It's there and, if anything, ignoring it only makes it grow larger. It's the side of your personality that you like to keep hidden in the dark.

Okay, no reason to be so dramatic about it. Yes, there are things about yourself, things you've thought and done, mistakes you've made, that you're not proud of. We are all alike in that way. Much of this can be addressed with what Jungian fans (they're out there) call Shadow Work. This post isn't specifically about that. I'm not your psychologist. If I were, you'd be in a lot of trouble. This blog post is merely an attempt to describe the shadow phenomenon in terms of the MBTI personality system. So let's open the trunk, shine the flashlight, and see what we've been avoiding for so long.

In my last post, I described my personality type, ISTP, using the car model. The shadow was described as the baggage for each person (cognitive function) being kept in the trunk. So I'll continue with my car model and describe the aspects of my shadow. This is only to describe how a shadow is formed. My deep dark secrets will still be my own. Be thankful.

So my cognitive stack is Introverted Thinking (Ti), Extroverted Sensing (Se), Introverted iNtuition (Ni), and Extroverted Feeling (Fe). My shadow functions are, in a way, mirror images of my cognitive functions. But they have the opposite focus. Just like your left and right are opposites to the right and left of your reflection in the mirror, your shadow functions oppose your cognitive functions.

So I have Extroverted Thinking (Te), Introverted Sensing (Si), Extroverted iNtuition (Ne), and Introverted Feeling (Fi) in my shadow personality type. This shadow cognitive stack matches the ESTJ personality type. Also my ISTP personality would match the shadow functions of a person with ESTJ preferences.

So what does this mean for me (and any interested person by extension)? While I cannot erase my past or go back and change things I've done, I can examine my shadow. I can know how it works and acknowledge parts of my personality that I may not like. Again, this is done in what's called Shadow Work, which has the makings of another future post. But for now, I can see my shadow.

Every cognitive function has good and bad aspects. Extroverted Thinking (Te) is great at creating systems that make things work. I like that, but it's also good at telling other people what to do. As an ISTP, not the biggest fan of that aspect. Into my shadow it goes. Introverted Sensing (Si) compares real time to past constructs. This function is a great memory booster, which is good. But it focuses on the past and the way things ought to be. ISTP's don't live in the past. We're in-the-moment people, so Si goes to the shadow. Extroverted iNtuition is the bane of my existence. I can't say anything good about it because it's in my blindspot. If you line all eight cognitive functions up from the primary function of the personality type to the final function in the shadow, the seventh function is the blindspot. Go figure. Definitely shadow material. Finally, Introverted Feeling (Fi) is a kind of filter that judges the outside world and decides," This is me," or, "This isn't me." There's certainly nothing wrong with that, ISTP's are not strong feelers. We don't like to live in our heads, at least not in that way. Feelings are irrational. Time to kick that whiny mess of a function into the shadow realm.

Don't misunderstand. Just because I don't like these things about myself, that doesn't mean they're not a part of me. Also, that doesn't mean the functions are bad or irrelevant. In both respects, they absolutely are.

I know how my shadow works. You should know how yours does too. This can help you to be at peace with yourself, because you don't defeat your shadow. You acknowledge it.

By the way, the ESTJ may be the shadow of my personality type, but that doesn't mean that the ESTJ is a bad personality type to have. That wouldn't be true at all. George Washington, the father of our country, is believed to have been an ESTJ. Where would we be today without his incredible leadership? And while I'm at it, I have to remember that my personality traits are a shadow to the ESTJ. This is hilarious to me in some ways, because I believe my father is an ESTJ (get under that bus, Dad). Strangely enough, the ISTP and the ESTJ are considered to be highly compatible personality types. It's a good thing too, because I work with my shadow type every day in a classroom full of kids. We get along just fine. There are scissors, staples, pushpins, and sharp pencils everywhere. Thank goodness, we have not maimed or even injured one kid yet.

*

Book(s) Review- The Paper Magician Novels

Charlie N. Holmberg is an author whom I follow on Amazon Kindle. Her (All of her sisters have boy names too.) work is a lot of fun to read. It's a turn of the century, post Victorian, slightly steampunk, magical world that is mostly based in England. Imagine magic being cultivated along side the Industrial Revolution. The series is whimsical when light and gritty when dark. It focuses on the relationship between a recently graduated apprentice of magic, Ceony, and her paper magician mentor, Emery.

There is a unique approach to magic in these books. Magic only works through man made materials. Ceony, much to her chagrin, has been forced to bond to paper. This is a life long bond. She can only use magic through paper. This means she will become a Folder, the least popular of all the magical disciplines. She dreamed of becoming a Smelter and working with metals. This is the beginning of an adventure that takes many turns that most readers would not expect.

Now the MBTI slant. If you are an ESTJ or are interested in the ESTJ point of view, these are the books for you. The main character, Ceony, is undoubtedly an ESTJ. This is plain to see from her inability to keep her mouth shut (according to herself) in the first chapter to her traditional love of cooking, which becomes a charming part of the story. Her eye for detail and what those details signify are crucial to the story and her personality as well. Her love of learning and applied logic to magic is evident in all three books. Her strong will (Judger) is what helps both her and her loved ones survive the trials of her adventures.

The three books featuring Ceony and her mentor, Emery Thane, are: THE PAPER MAGICIAN, THE GLASS MAGICIAN, and THE MASTER MAGICIAN. There is a fourth book related to this series titled, THE PLASTIC MAGICIAN, in which the two main characters have brief cameo appearances.

*

The Imposter Nurse

Denise Compton's book, THE IMPOSTER NURSE, is based on a true story. It happened back in the seventies, so it was like getting in a time machine for me, because I was born in that decade. The story is about a wife and mother named Angie who gets a new job at a nursing home as a nurse's aid. In this new environment, suspicious activities begin occurring. Angie has to make some tough decisions.

This story is a great read for the ISTJ, which is what I believe to be the main character's personality type. Given the monicker, The Inspector, the ISTJ is respectful of the rules and can smell when something isn't quite right. This doesn't mean they are nosy at all, but they do usually have a strong moral core and are not afraid to stand up for what's right.

What I liked best about the book was all the sensory details that could only come from an adult living in that era. It was fascinating for me to view the time of my early childhood through the eyes of a wife, mother, and medical professional.

The story takes some surprising turns. Real life is always stranger than fiction. In fact, you could say that the plot literally turns on a dime. Not being an overly long read, two or three sittings, the story is well worth your time.

*

Just One Letter?

During this COVID19 interruption, I've caught up on some TV watching. One show that I've enjoyed is Grimm, which originally aired on NBC (I think). It's a fantasy series based on the classic folk tales from the Brothers Grimm. The story mostly takes place in Portland, Oregon. I like watching shows that have already run their course because it's often like reading a good book. This show ran five seasons, which is a pretty good investment for your binge watching. One thing that I really liked was the surprising depth of characters. With that in mind, two supporting characters, Monroe an Trubel (yes, pronounced as trouble), are great examples of how just one letter in the MBTI personality system makes a huge difference.

Monroe is probably an ISFP, nicknamed The Artist. Trubel, actually Theresa Rubel, is a likely ISTP. This type is known as The Crafter or the Virtuoso. So what happens when you go from an F to a T or vice versa? Quite a lot actually.

Monroe's lead cognitive function is Introverted Feeling (Fi). He makes decisions based on his own inner values. He's all about his core beliefs. Trubel's lead function is Introverted Thinking (Ti). She makes her decision's based on logic, which can be subjective or objective, but is always seeking truth and can be cold and hard. They both have Extroverted Sensing (Se) as their second function, which plants them firmly in reality (though it's a fantasy series) in comparison to the theory exploring intuitive types. The differences between the two play out well in the show.

Monroe is a Blutbad, which is a kind of Big Bad Wolf monster man, though he will be the first to tell you he's reformed. His character is quirky and artistic. He's fascinated by obscure classical composers and is an avid cellist himself. His career of choice is clock repair, of which he is a compassionate advocate. This character is also a Pilates buff (speaking of core values) and lover of holidays, especially Christmas and Halloween. Though he doesn't shirk from wolfing out and tearing bad guys apart (literally), he's quite warm a fuzzy. An interesting depth of emotional intelligence comes with Monroe's development too. His well developed Fi can be seen through his loyalty to the main character, a Grimm who is supposed to be his mortal enemy. Likewise, his love to the point of near death (a trial by fire episode) for his wife Rosalee, who is a different type of Wessen (pronounced Vessen), is a steadfast Fi-centric trait. Their marriage is considered taboo by some in the underworld community, which leads to a kind of supernatural civil rights conflict in the plot.

Trubel comes to the show in the the third season. She is a young Grimm who is taken in by the main character. Her Ti/Se personality fits the ISTP stereotypes perfectly. She inadvertently says awkward, blunt things, which is due to her undeveloped Extroverted Feeling (Fe). Also her tender, daughter like feelings for Nick, the main Grimm, often take her by surprise. She is cold and calculated, but physically formidable, with catlike reflexes allowing her to take on and engage multiple enemies. She naturally takes on the Grimm Wessen assassin role. Unlike the deep-feeling Monroe, she makes her decisions based on logic, which allows her to even kill a major character in the show that she and all her friends loved at one point. It was the right thing to do, but a decision that could only be made by an ISTP.

If you like fantasy or (mild) horror TV, Grimm is a good show to check out. All the characters are well developed from the ENTJ police captain to the XSTJ girlfriend. There is plenty of intrigue and action. The CGI is a little clunky, but improves as the show continues. Some Wessen are more striking than others. I personally don't like the sheep and rabbit creations, but the plot is good and interesting. One thing that I like about this show, other than the characters, is that the Big Boss plot line never takes over the show. There is always a murder case to be solved in most episodes of every season, which keeps things flowing.

*

In summary, I recommend that teachers learn about MBTI, especially the cognitive functions. There is no need to go around typing kids. In fact, almost everyone in the MBTI community would advise against that. But understanding personality is understanding people. Isn't that who we are teaching? Seems to me it would be pretty darn important to understand whom as well as what we are teaching.

Don't miss out!

Visit the website below and you can sign up to receive emails whenever Jon Coley publishes a new book. There's no charge and no obligation.

https://books2read.com/r/B-A-OVTX-FSMKC

BOOKS2READ

Connecting independent readers to independent writers.

Did you love *From the Peanuts Section: Personality Psychology and Pop Culture*? Then you should read *Numbskulls: Navigating Personality Conflicts*[1] by Jon Coley!

We've all been there ...

Dealing with that obstinate coworker ...

Or that overbearing family member ...

Explore personality differences in this short book to discover why we sometimes have difficulty getting along with one another. Not only that, but also find out what you can do about it. Learn how to give yourself (and others) a little grace as you endeavor to navigate those choppy waters.

Read more at www.joncoleyauthor.substack.com.

---

1. https://books2read.com/u/baBG22

2. https://books2read.com/u/baBG22

Also by Jon Coley

Schooling Abraham
Tickled to Death: Funny Epitaphs for Kids
Numbskulls: Navigating Personality Conflicts
Anthology of Seasons
Skate or Die Jacob Jones
The Not So Great Divide
The Echo Chamber
Are You Kidding Me?
All Grandpas Fish
From the Peanuts Section: Personality Psychology and Pop Culture
The Other Curse of Mr. M's Castle
The Western Weird
The Curse of Mr. M's Castle
The Ghost of Dream Gully
The Fish Creek Forum Volume 1
The Bookworm
Limerick City
Bloody Bones
You Tryna Be Funny? Jokes for Kids

Watch for more at www.joncoleyauthor.substack.com.

About the Author

Jon Coley lives in Georgia with his wife, daughters, an orange cat, an eccentric husky, and an overly affectionate a Great Dane. He has been a school teacher for more than twenty-five years. That's probably what's wrong with him..

Read more at www.joncoleyauthor.substack.com.

www.ingramcontent.com/pod-product-compliance
Lightning Source LLC
Chambersburg PA
CBHW031757150726
47989CB00006B/2759